1

by Marlene LeFever
illustrated by Kathleen Weyna

CHARIOT BOOKS
from David C. Cook Publishing Co.

Elgin, Illinois 60120
Weston, Ontario

CREATIVE KIDS - 1

First printing, 1984

Printed in the United States of America

89 88 87 86 85 84   5 4 3 2 1

ISBN 0-89191-935-X

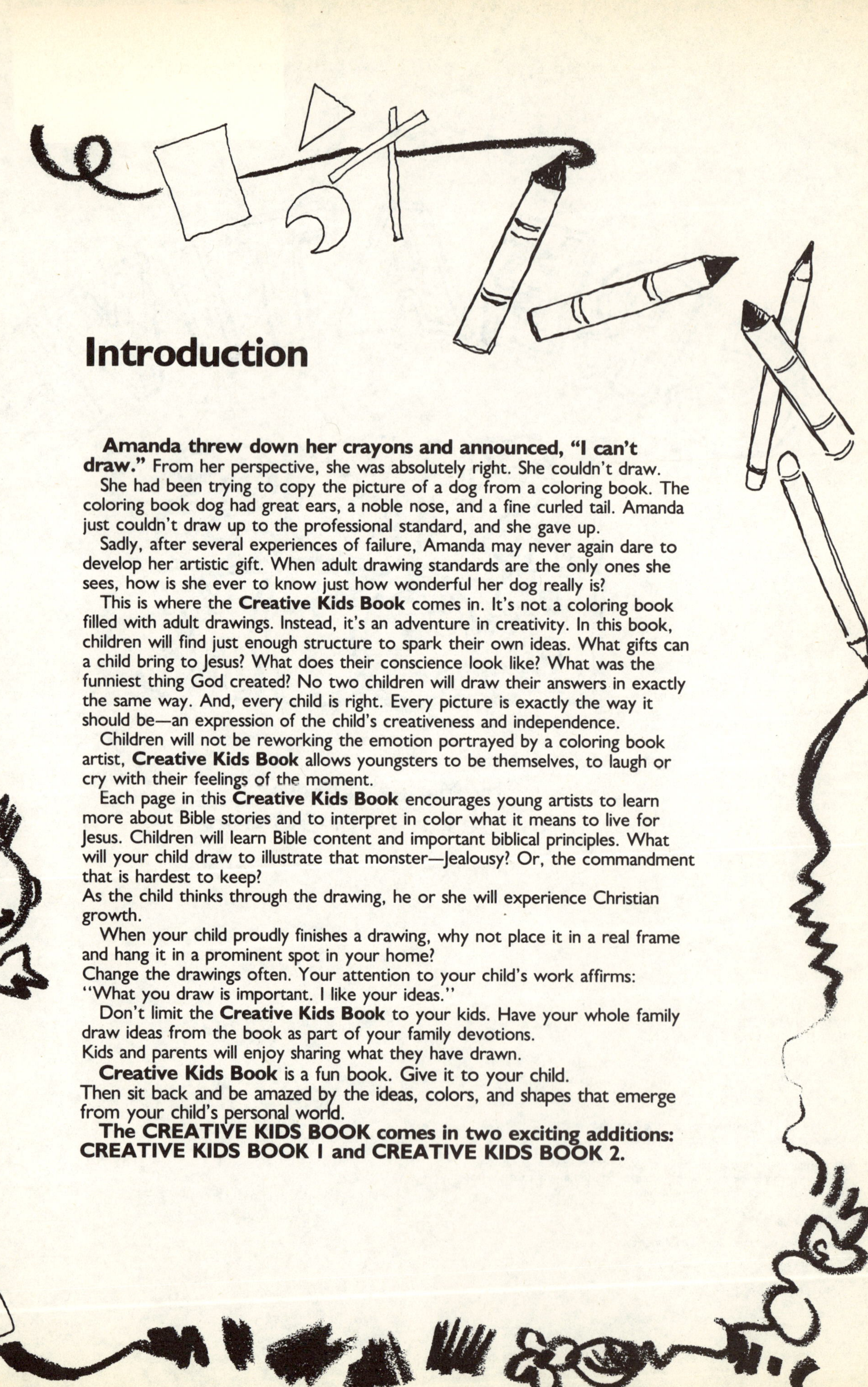

Introduction

Amanda threw down her crayons and announced, "I can't draw." From her perspective, she was absolutely right. She couldn't draw.

She had been trying to copy the picture of a dog from a coloring book. The coloring book dog had great ears, a noble nose, and a fine curled tail. Amanda just couldn't draw up to the professional standard, and she gave up.

Sadly, after several experiences of failure, Amanda may never again dare to develop her artistic gift. When adult drawing standards are the only ones she sees, how is she ever to know just how wonderful her dog really is?

This is where the **Creative Kids Book** comes in. It's not a coloring book filled with adult drawings. Instead, it's an adventure in creativity. In this book, children will find just enough structure to spark their own ideas. What gifts can a child bring to Jesus? What does their conscience look like? What was the funniest thing God created? No two children will draw their answers in exactly the same way. And, every child is right. Every picture is exactly the way it should be—an expression of the child's creativeness and independence.

Children will not be reworking the emotion portrayed by a coloring book artist, **Creative Kids Book** allows youngsters to be themselves, to laugh or cry with their feelings of the moment.

Each page in this **Creative Kids Book** encourages young artists to learn more about Bible stories and to interpret in color what it means to live for Jesus. Children will learn Bible content and important biblical principles. What will your child draw to illustrate that monster—Jealousy? Or, the commandment that is hardest to keep?
As the child thinks through the drawing, he or she will experience Christian growth.

When your child proudly finishes a drawing, why not place it in a real frame and hang it in a prominent spot in your home?
Change the drawings often. Your attention to your child's work affirms: "What you draw is important. I like your ideas."

Don't limit the **Creative Kids Book** to your kids. Have your whole family draw ideas from the book as part of your family devotions.
Kids and parents will enjoy sharing what they have drawn.

Creative Kids Book is a fun book. Give it to your child.
Then sit back and be amazed by the ideas, colors, and shapes that emerge from your child's personal world.

The CREATIVE KIDS BOOK comes in two exciting additions: CREATIVE KIDS BOOK 1 and CREATIVE KIDS BOOK 2.

Draw a pattern on 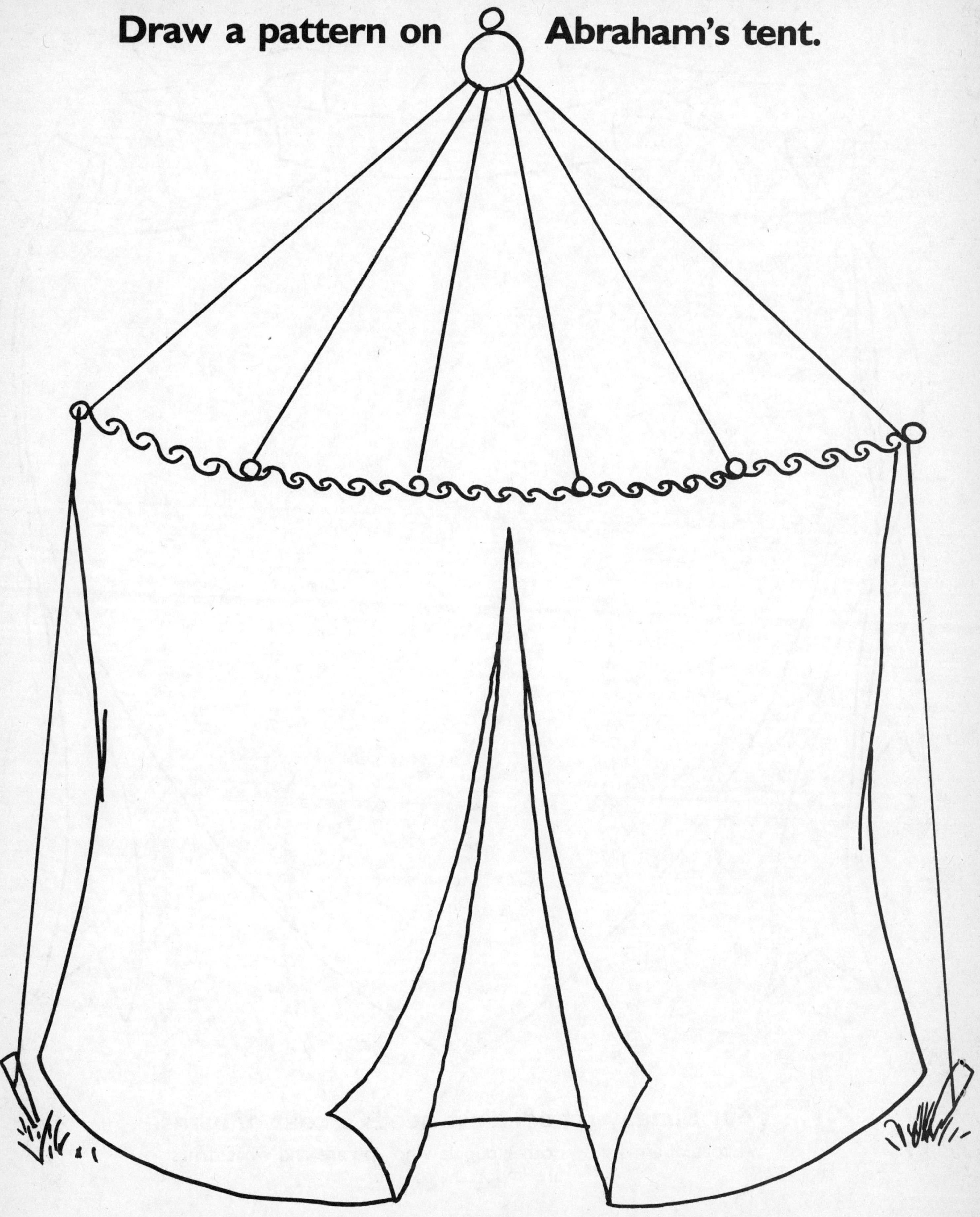 Abraham's tent.

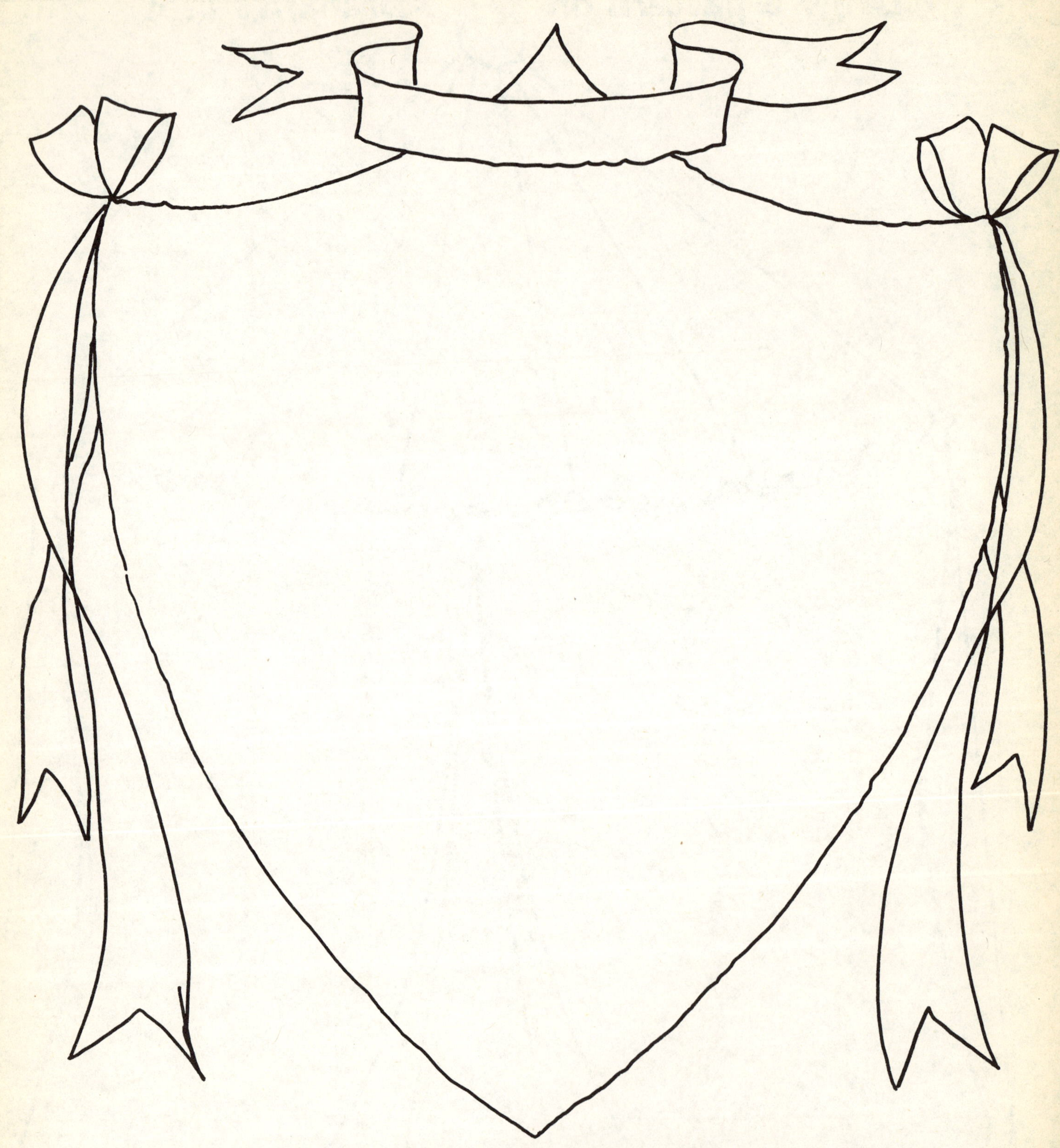

Your Sunday school class needs a coat of arms.

A coat of arms shows other people who you are and what things
are important to you.

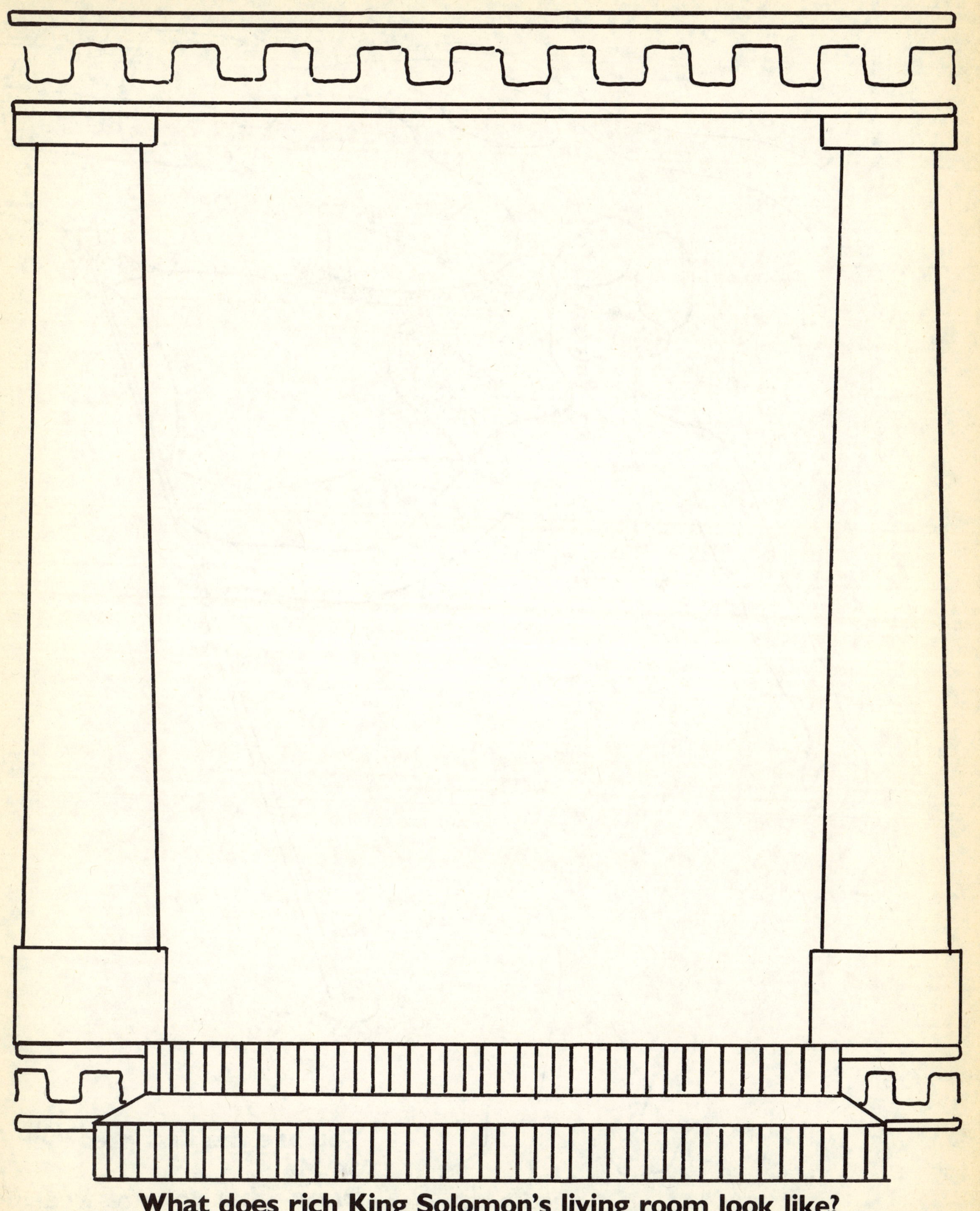

What does rich King Solomon's living room look like?

Read I Kings 4:29-34 to find out more about this important king.

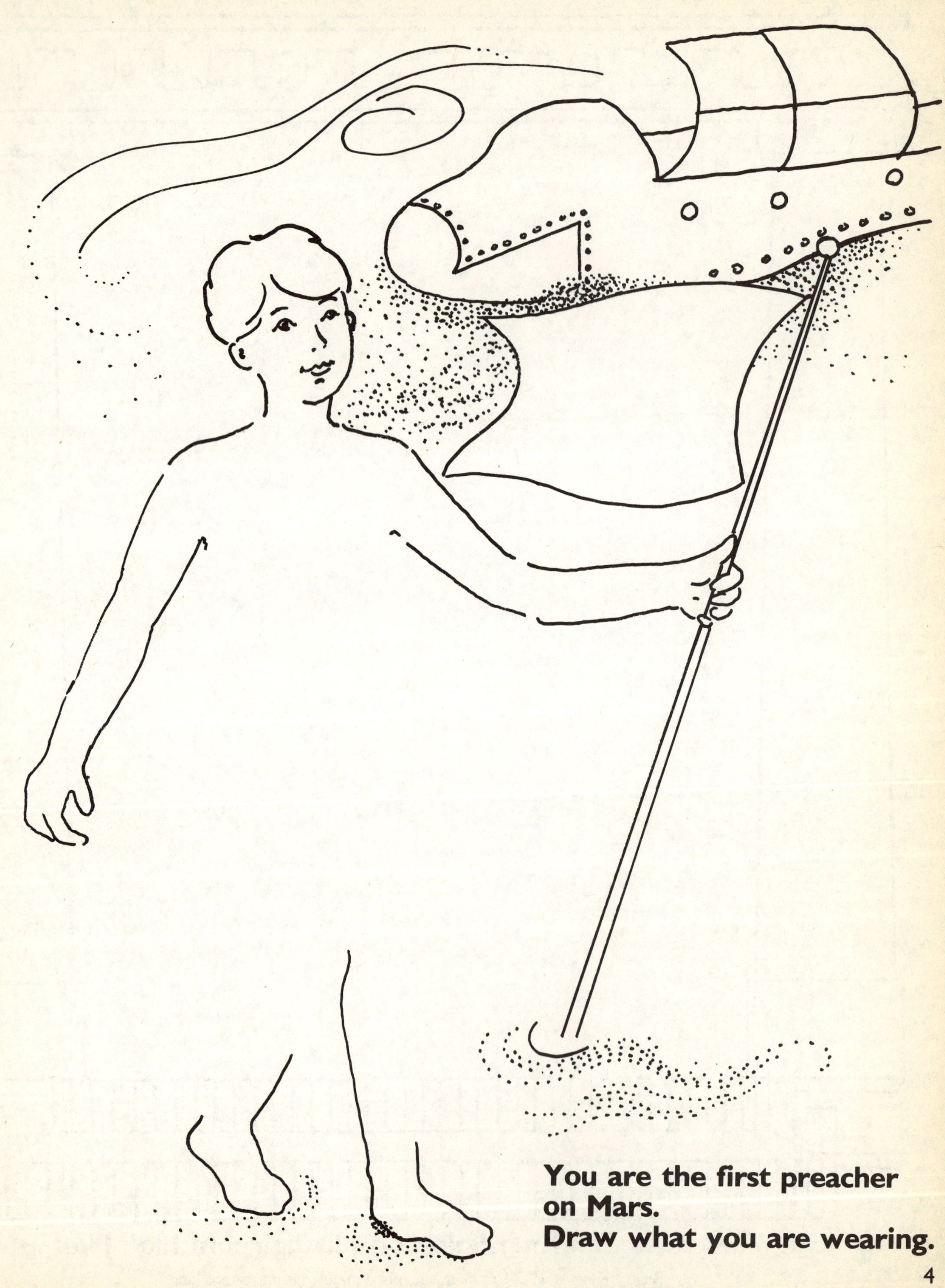

**You are the first preacher
on Mars.
Draw what you are wearing.**

You build a steeple for your church.

Queen Esther needs a beautiful dress.

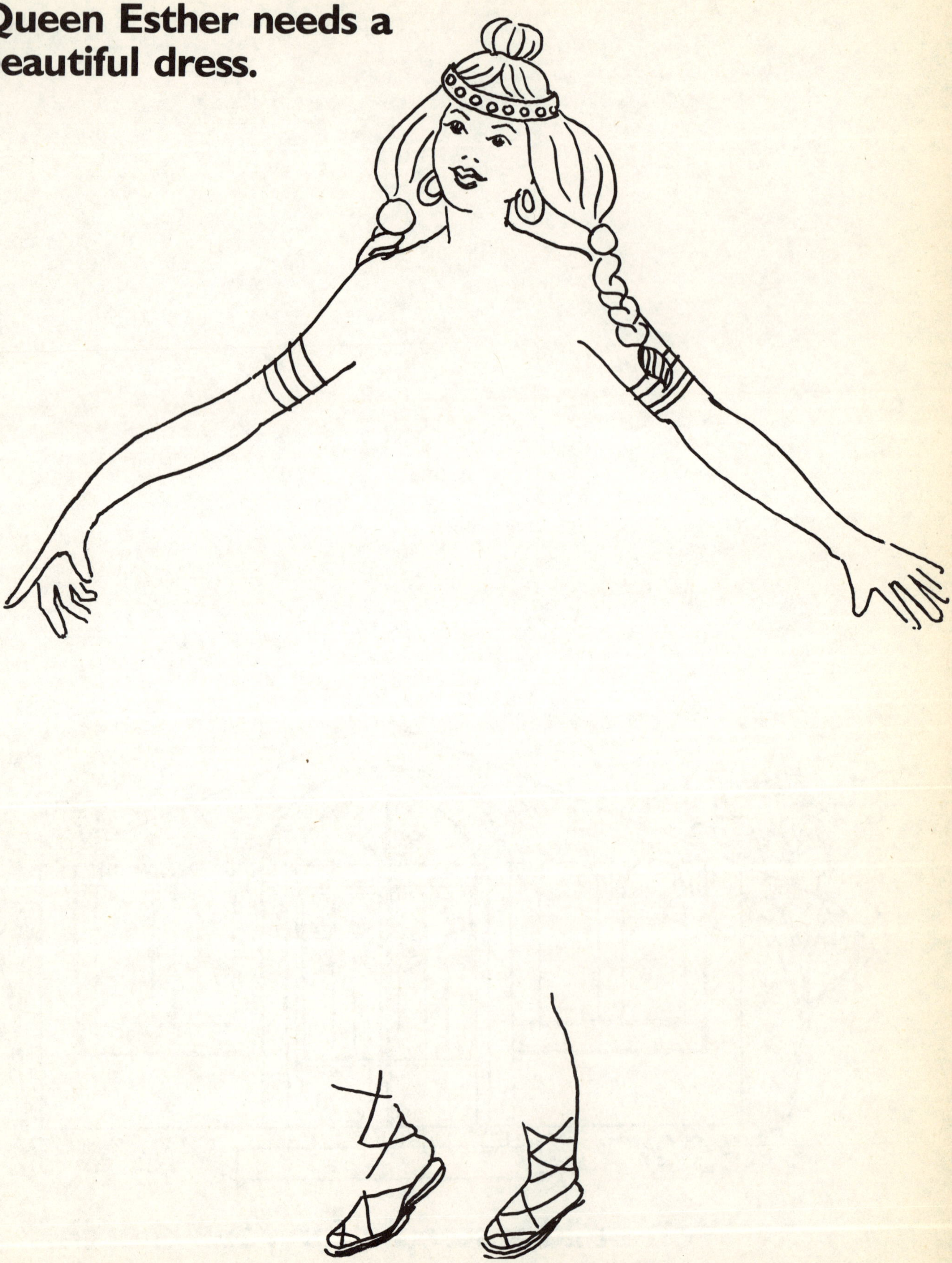

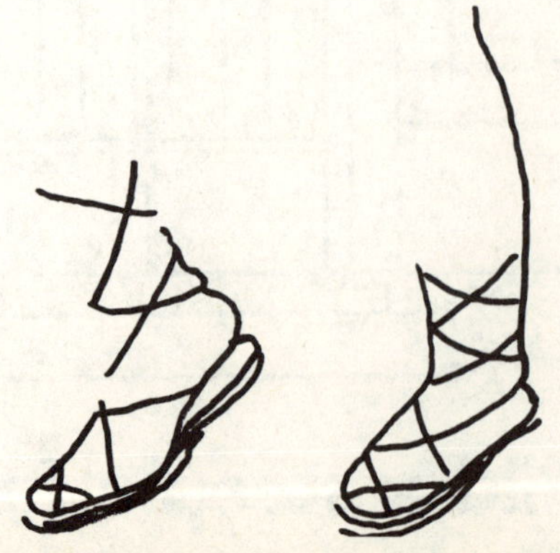

God used Esther to save her Jewish people from being murdered.

Make a Christian Easter card to send to your friends.

Mark 16:1-10 tells about the first Easter.

Draw the funniest thing God created.

Get some ideas from Genesis 1:20-25.

You have been asked to draw a Christian postage stamp.
It should show something important about Jesus.

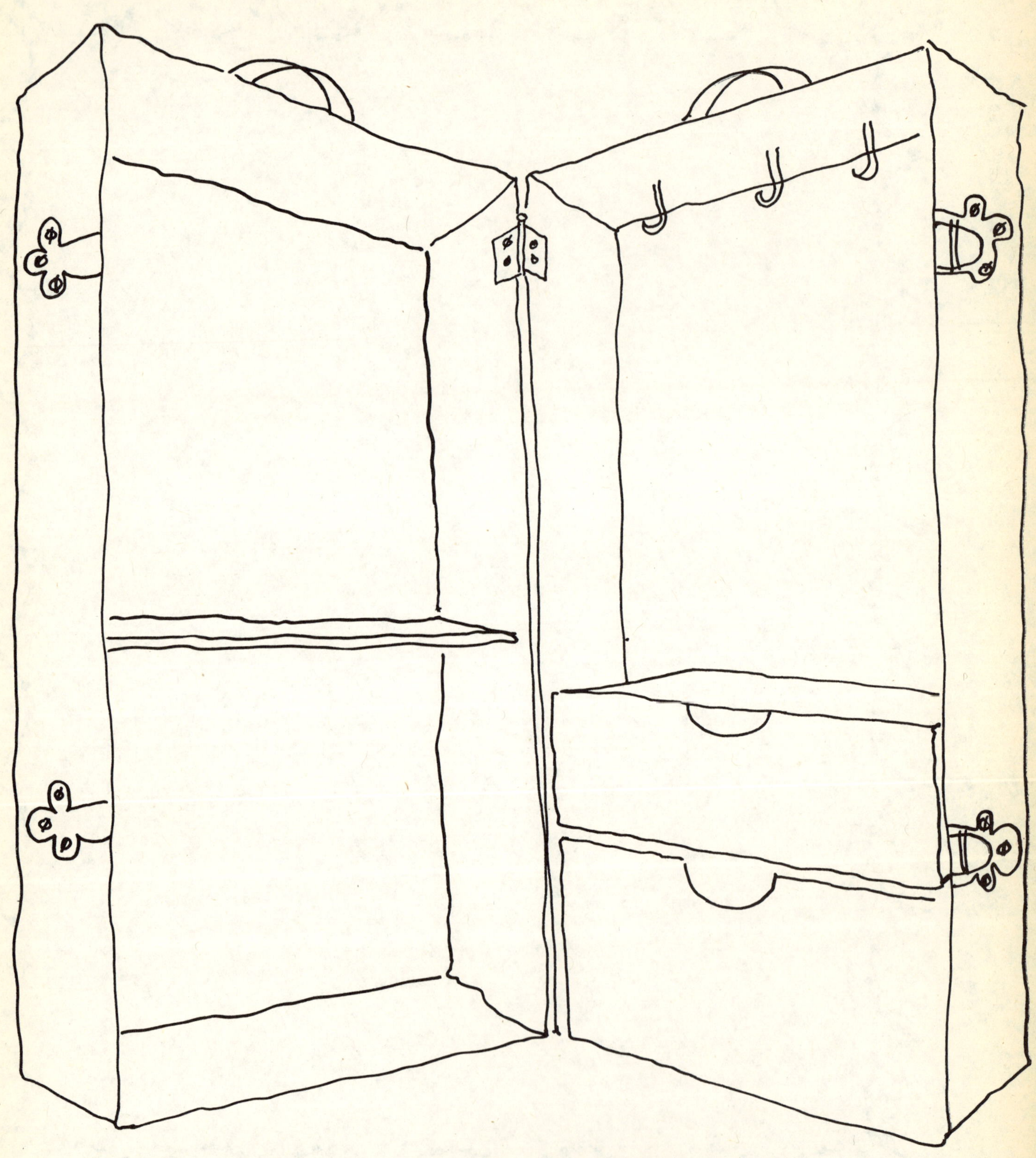

**You are going on a missionary journey with Paul.
Pack three things to take with you.**

Acts 13:3-5 will tell you a little about Paul's work for Jesus.

**Make a patchwork quilt
from Christian symbols or pictures.**

You are an archaeologist digging near Jerusalem. What will you find?

An archaeologist looks for pots, tools, and even whole cities.
These things help us know more about people who lived long ago.

Dress Jacob the way the Bible tells us he dressed to trick his father.

You'll need to read Genesis 25:27-34; 27:1-29.

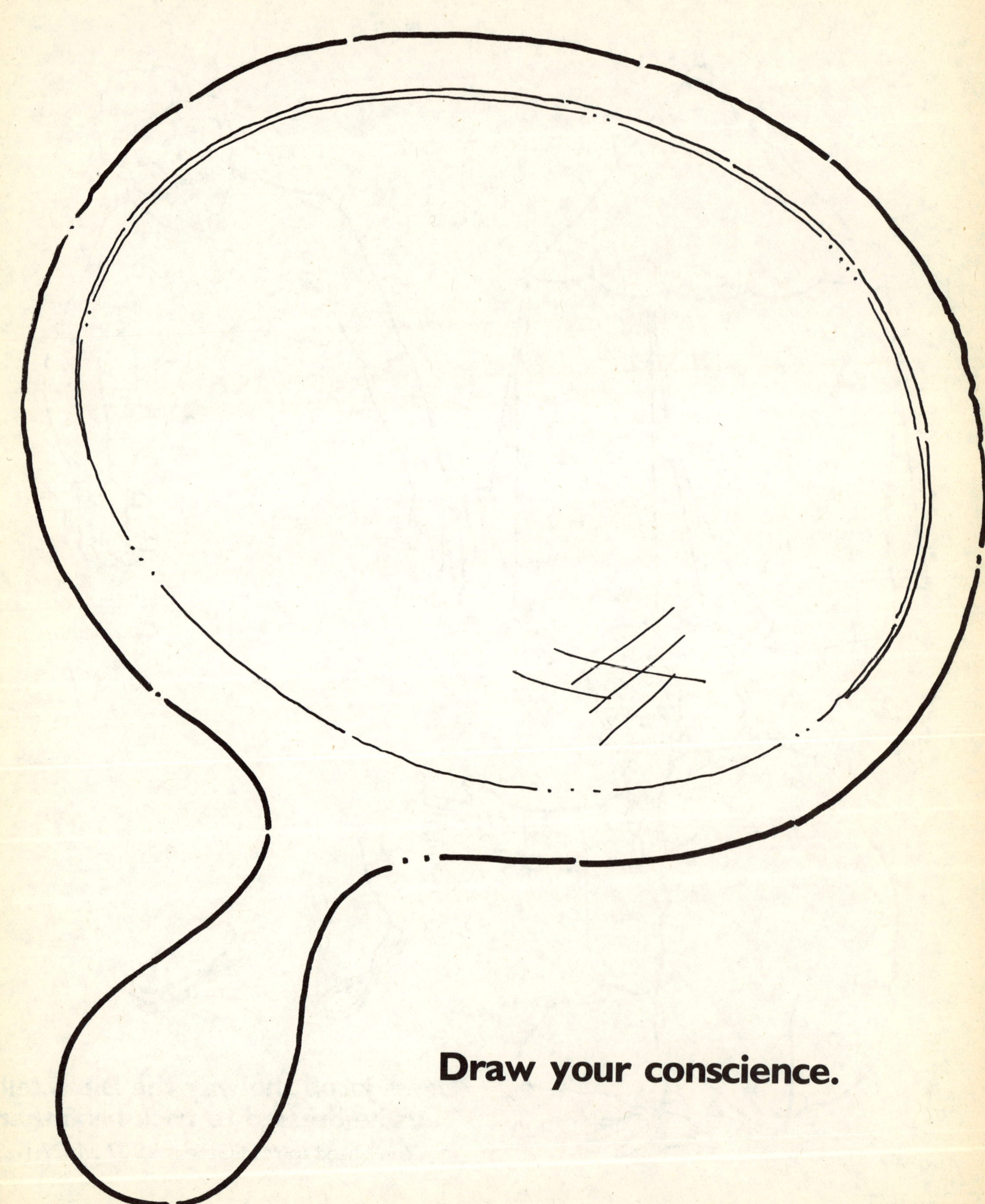

Draw your conscience.

Make a movie of the fall of the walls of Jericho.

Read Joshua 6:2-20 before you start your movie.

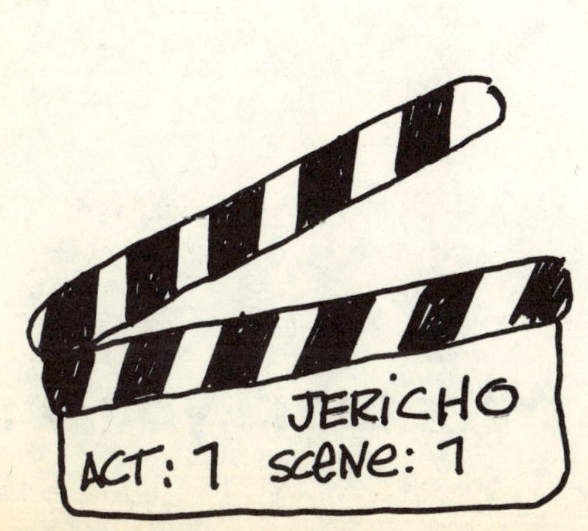

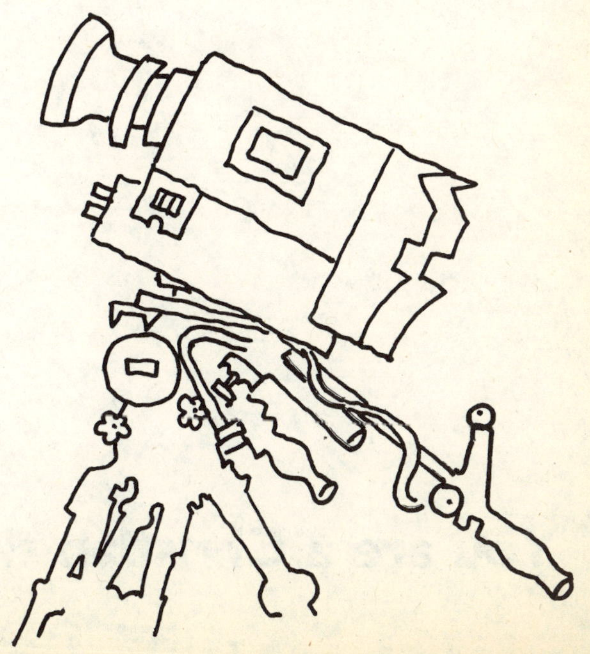

You are a Christian skywriter. What will you write?

Picture a Bible story that would make a great TV series.

For hints, think about the people in Exodus 2:10;
I Samuel 17:41, 42; Luke 2:52; and Acts 9:22.

What does an angel really look like?

What kind of food do you think Joseph served his brothers? He loved them even though they had sold him as a slave.

Read Genesis 43:25-34.

Plant flowers and trees in the garden where Jesus was buried.
Read Luke 23:50-55.

MONSTER SIGHTED

Draw the Monster Jealousy!

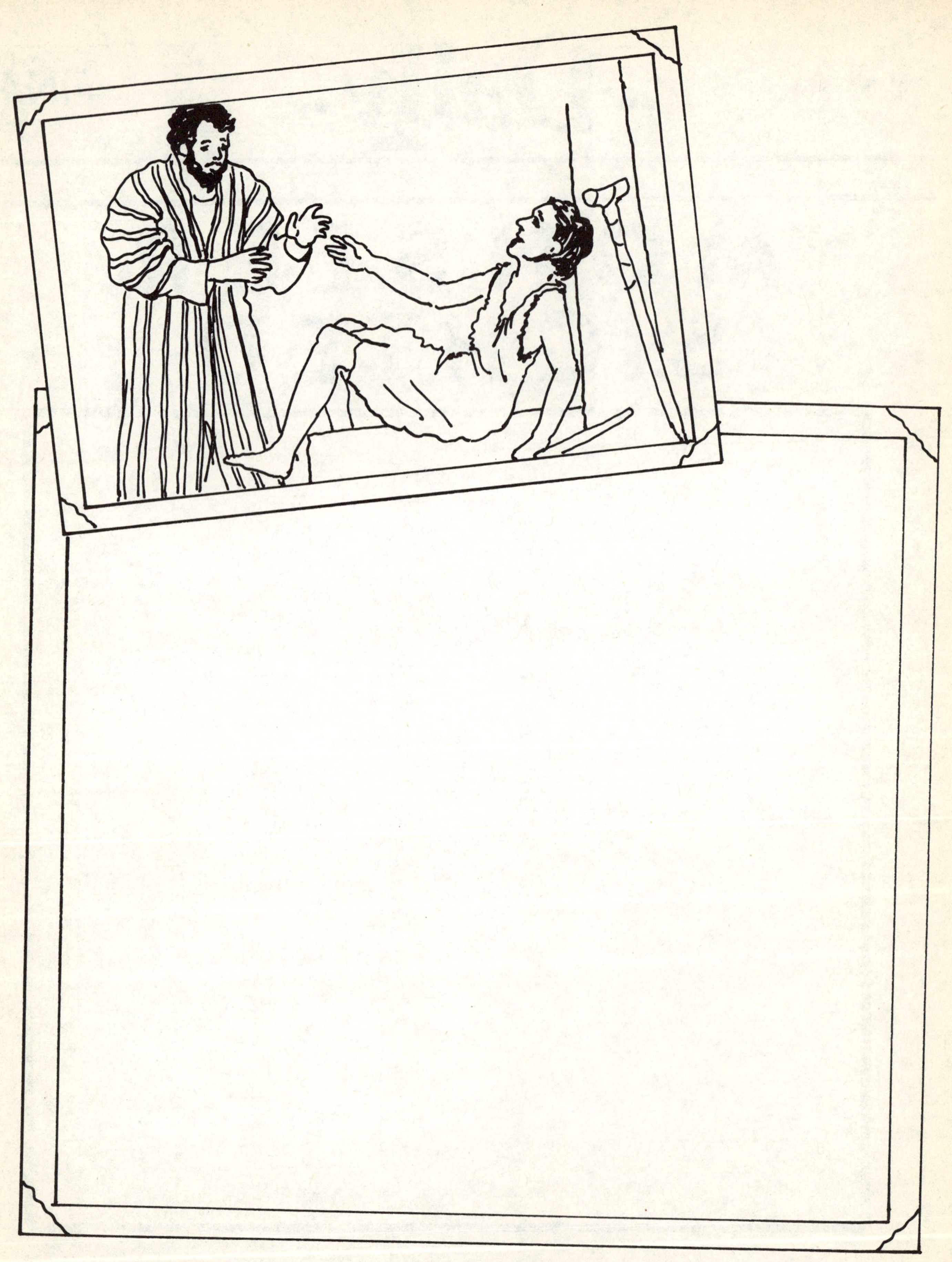

Whoopie! Draw the lame man 10 minutes after this picture was taken. Don't forget to read Acts 3:1-8.

Draw your favorite Bible story,
and hang it on your wall.

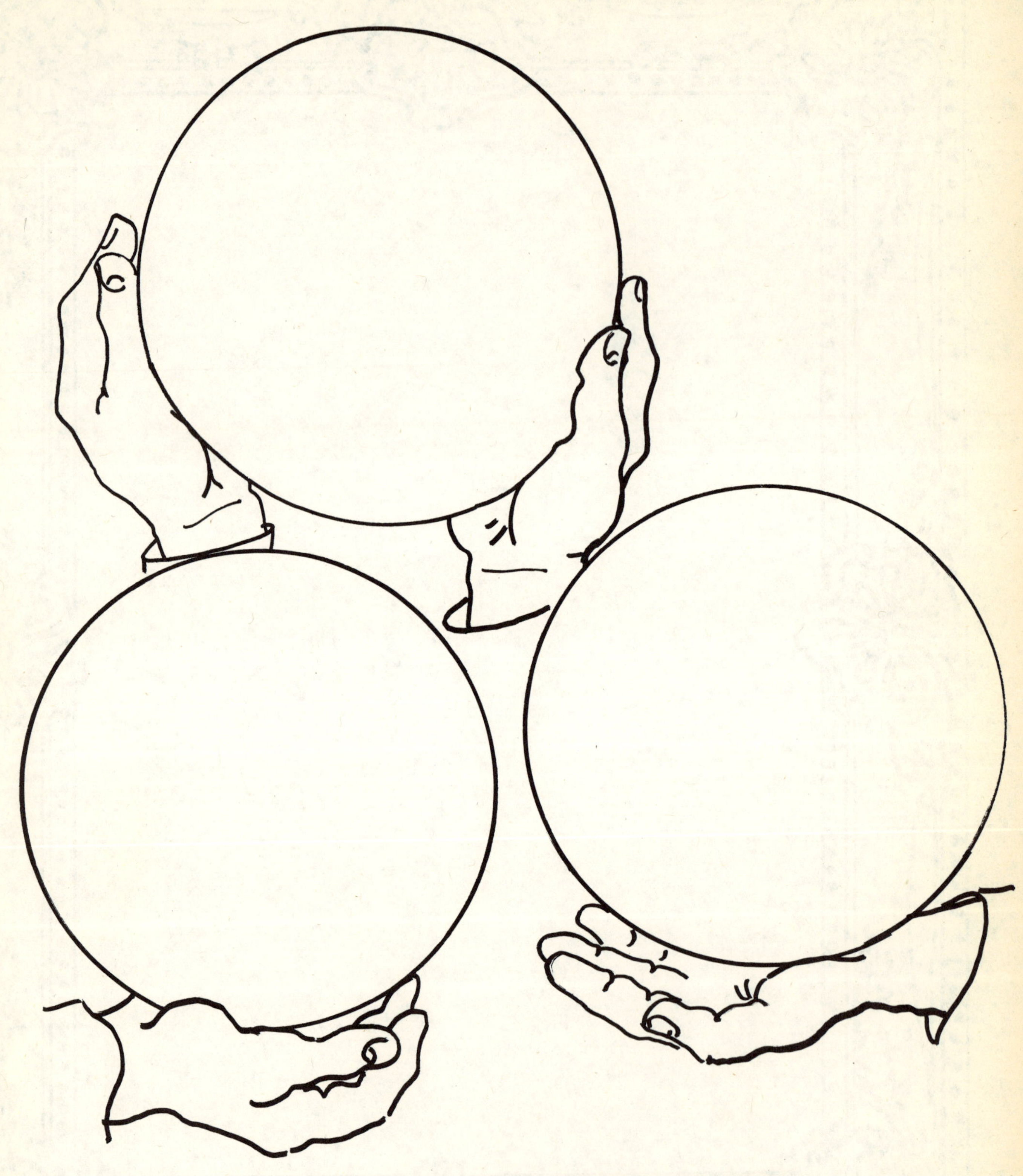

The Wise Men brought gifts to Jesus.
What gifts can you bring to Jesus?

Make a Christian T-shirt.

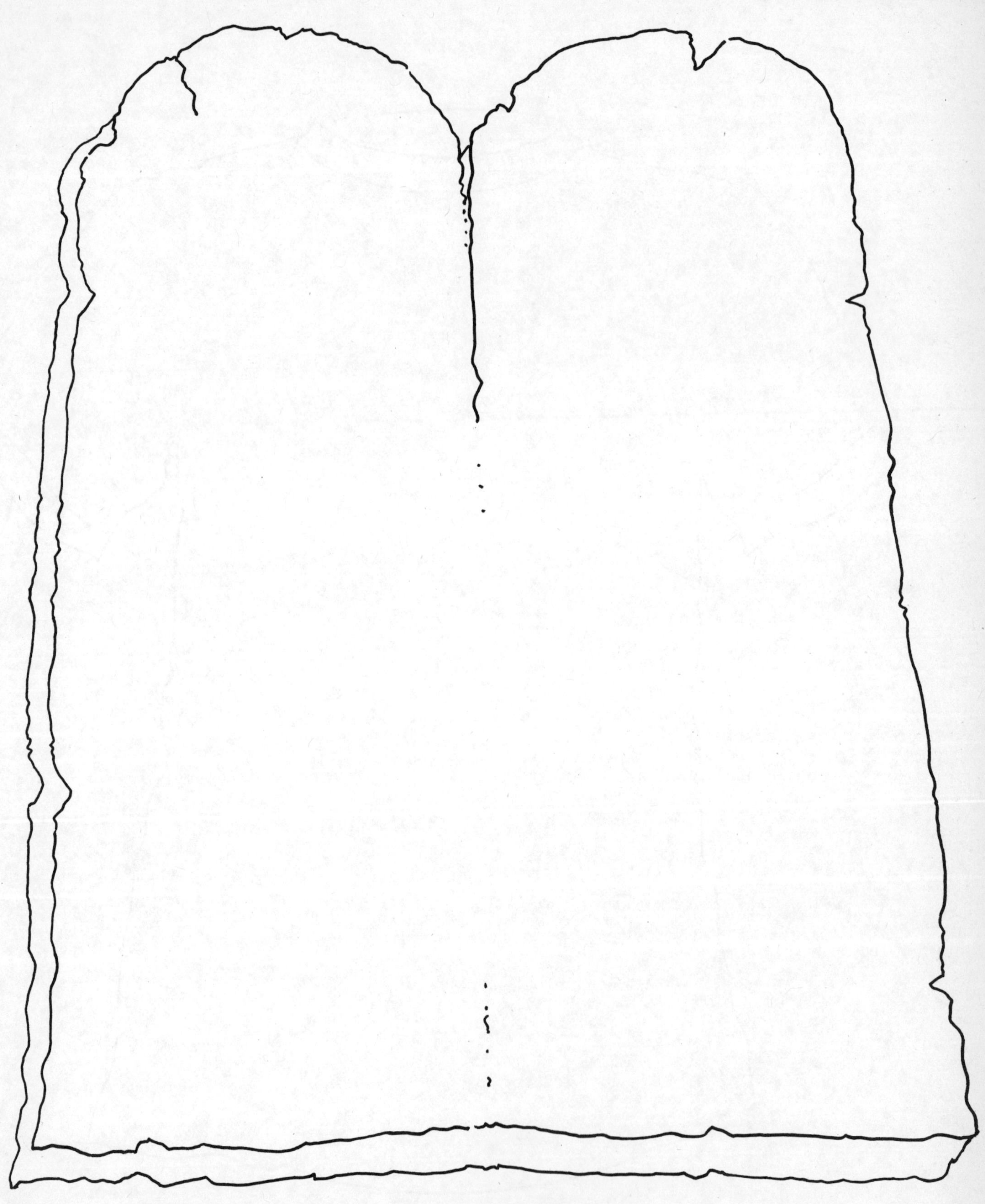

Read the Ten Commandments in Exodus 20:3-17.

Picture the commandment that is the hardest for you.

BEFORE...
Samson before
his haircut.

AFTER!
Samson after
his haircut.
The sad story is in
Judges 15:20; 16:4-21.

Draw your answer to the question, "What is sin?"

Draw why 8 of the 10 spies were scared to go into the Promised Land —even when God told them they should.
Numbers 13:27, 28 will give you the answer.

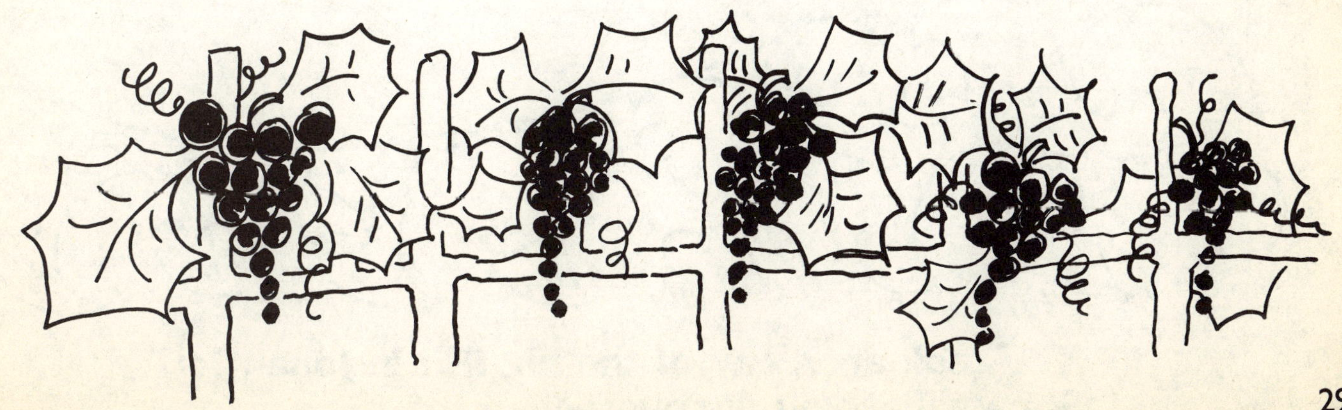

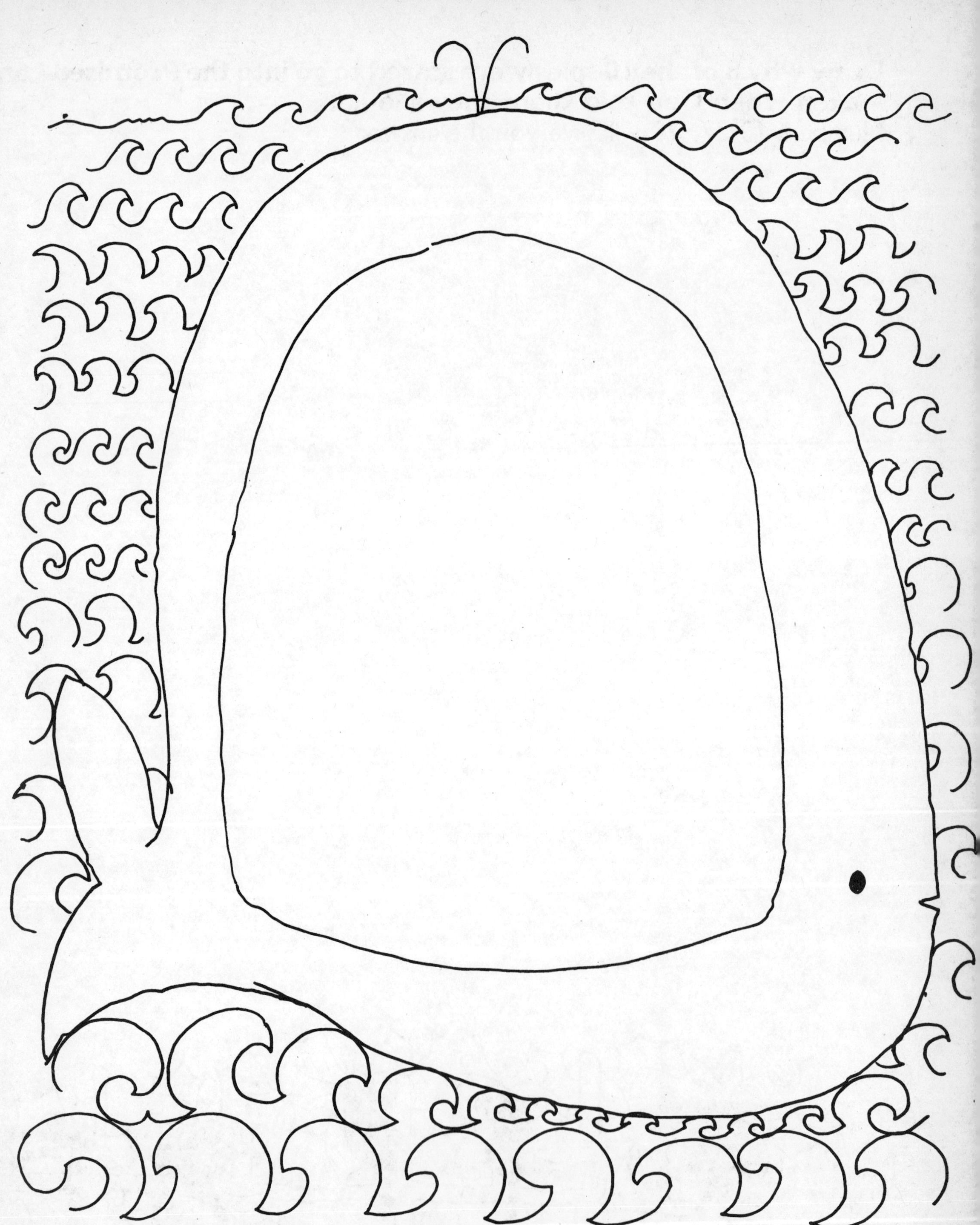

**You took an X ray of the big fish in Jonah 1:17.
Show what you discovered.**